Mexico City

THE FOOD ENTHUSIAST'S COMPLETE RESTAURANT GUIDE
2019

Andrew Delaplaine

*Andrew Delaplaine is the Food Enthusiast.
When he's not playing tennis, he dines anonymously
at the Publisher's (considerable) expense.*

Senior Editors – Renee & Sophie Delaplaine
Senior Writer – James Cubby
Art Director – Chip McGoldrick

Gramercy Park Press
New York – London – Paris

Copyright © by Gramercy Park Press - All rights reserved.

Please submit corrections, additions or comments to
gppress@gmail.com

The Food Enthusiast's Complete Restaurant Guide

Table of Contents

Introduction – 5

Getting About – 11

The A to Z Listings – 19
Ridiculously Extravagant
Sensible Alternatives
Quality Bargain Spots

Nightlife – 57

Index – 63

Other Books by the Food Enthusiast – 67

INTRODUCTION

I love Mexico City, even though the first time I traveled there, with my mother, we almost brought her back in a box. She had made the mistake of using the ice cubes in her hotel room fridge to make a drink instead of pouring bottled water into the ice trays.
Boom!
You're sick as a dog.
But that was many years ago. Generally, I've had

nothing but wonderful times in Mexico City.

When I think about what Mexico City was and how it came to be what it is today, my mind still boggles.

You have to remember that the whole city is built on a drained lake bed. When there was still a lake, around 1325, it was established as the Aztec capital called Tenochititlán. The island in the middle of the lake was reached by way of a series of causeways. This was what Hernan Cortes found when he showed up in 1521. He promptly destroyed it.

Mexico has a rich and bloody history, not unlike all the other countries in the New World where the indigenous populations where slaughtered or enslaved. (But one has to remember that Cortes didn't do anything to the Aztecs that the English settlers didn't do to the Indians.)

The altitude is high, over 7,000 feet, so if you come from a low-lying coastal area, be prepared for some difficulty in breathing. And while the government has made enormous strides in cleaning up the famously polluted air in Mexico City, it's still pretty awful. You have to pray for good air. But you can never be sure of it.

There are things about Mexico in general that you want to be aware of if you want to travel wisely—and safely. The State Department says 14 of the 31 states (and Federal District, or *Distrito Federal*, or D.F., which is Mexico City) have no travel warnings. The others you want to avoid because of the drug-related gang warfare that's an ongoing reality in Mexico, responsible for ripping the country apart. (Americans are really to blame, since we're the ones buying all the drugs.)

One of the reasons Mexico City is so much more safe than other parts of the country is that everybody wants to be able to come here and visit it in peace, and this includes a lot of the high-end drug dealers, many of whom have houses and families here. They don't want to come here and duel it out on the streets the way they do elsewhere.

Of the 20 top foreign locations for Americans, 4 are in Mexico: No. 2 is Cancun, followed by No. 3, Playa del Carmen, Cabo san Lucas / Los Cabos at No. 11 and Puerto Vallarta at No. 15.

One good thing about Mexico City is that it has been sidestepped by the drug cartels so there's no sense of the overwhelming violence that occurs in other parts of Mexico.

You will find the *Distrito Federal* (Federal District, another name for the city) to be quite a beautiful, handsomely laid-out city.

Lay of the Land

At 571 square miles, D.F.—as Mexico City residents, or *chilangos*, call it—is vast, but visitors gravitate to a few key neighborhoods.

Centro Histórico: Anchored by the Zócalo plaza, the historic center is a mix of monuments and bustling commerce.

Roma: Hipsters, artists, and boutique owners

have revived this once-bourgeois neighborhood of Art Nouveau mansions.

Condesa: In Mexico City's answer to New York's West Village, shops, restaurants, and apartments radiate out from the Parque México.

Polanco: One of the city's poshest districts keeps expanding north: "Nuevo Polanco" is being colonized by galleries and shopping malls.

Getting Around Safely: Taxis are plentiful, but you may feel more secure having a private car. From Journey Mexico at www.journeymexico.com

For the latest safety information, go to the U.S. State Department at travel.state.gov.

CASH & DEBIT CARDS.

Notify the companies whose cards you use that you are going to Mexico. Transactions might be blocked if you don't. Have them send you alerts or call you if any charge looks suspicious. When using ATMs, try to avoid street side ATMs in favor of ATMS inside a bank or other business.

Have credit card numbers and other information written down in a safe place.

You'll need cash because a lot of places don't accept plastic. But get your currency converted before going to Mexico because you'll stick out as a foreigner by getting it done at the airport when you land. (The rates are high there too.) A lot of currency exchange booths are not in secure areas, so beware.

YOUR DRESS.
You're not in Vegas, you're in a potentially dangerous city, so leave the shorts and flip-flops at home unless you're visiting the beach somewhere. Don't be an obvious tourist. Keep your camera in your travel bag, not around your neck.

YOUR PHONE.
Don't be glued to it the way so many people are, not when you're out on the streets. You're begging for trouble.

Check with your carrier to find out what the fees are when traveling in Mexico.

TAXIS.
See below.

GETTING ABOUT

There's an extensive Metro system, a bus system, a trolley system. I would avoid them all unless you *really* know your way around. I never use them. Never.

They even have special cars on the Metro system for women only because women get groped on the mixed cars. Also there's the constant threat of pickpockets. Stay way.

Mexico City is one of the world's largest cities and boasts an estimated population of 21 million people living in the region. Mexico City is divided into 16 areas known as delegaciones, not unlike New York's boroughs. These areas are further divided into neighborhoods called "colonias" and there are about 250 of these.

When traveling the city, it is important to know which colonia that you're traveling to and be aware that some have duplicate or very similar names. Visitors to Mexico City need to take note of the increase in crime and safety concerns that are prevalent in the city.

While traveling throughout Mexico City by public transportation can be economical, it is not always the safest mode of transportation and warnings regarding use of public transportation should be respected.

Locals and those familiar with Mexico City travel freely and cheaply via the Metro, first- and second-class buses.

However, visitors should travel by ***sitio taxis*** (official taxis registered to a specific locale or hotel), as these taxis are fairly inexpensive and the safest means of travel within the city.

"Turismo" and Sitio Taxis

These two methods are the safest means of travel within Mexico City. Turismo taxis, un-marked cabs, are usually luxury cars that are assigned to specific hotels and are identified by their special license plates. These may be more expensive that other taxis but they are the safest.

Established rates are fixed for travel to and from the airport. However, rates for traveling to other destinations and sightseeing need to be negotiated with the drivers.

The bell captain at your hotel can tell you what the airport fare should be and make sure to confirm with the cab driver before departure. Theses cab drivers, usually licensed English-speaking guides, can be excellent tour guides and provide valuable information regarding Mexico City.

While these cabs usually charge around 15% more than metered rates, the price is well worth it as these drivers can wait for you while you dine or shop or will pick you up when you call.

Getting Around Safely: Taxis are plentiful, but you may feel more secure having a private car. From Journey Mexico at www.journeymexico.com

Metered Taxis

Some sitio taxis (radio taxis) are safe and use meters, others have fixed rates. Travelers need to be cautious as some drivers will overcharge passengers, advance the meter, or even drive farther than requested to run up the tab. One recommended safe radio taxi service is **55 5590 3325** or **55 6898 5192.**

Do not hail a taxi. A lot of the drivers are unlicensed, illegal and unsafe.

Your hotel will call a reputable taxi for you, a "radio taxi." If you're in a restaurant and ready to leave at night, have them call a cab for you.

If you're out on the street and need a cab, go into a nearby hotel or restaurant and have them call for you. Or go to a taxi stand, labeled *Sitio de Taxi,* where real tcxis will be located. These are designated taxis and OK to use. These maroon and gold Nissans are slightly more expensive than the green *libre* taxis, but much more secure.

Metro

The Mexico City subway offers one of the cheapest fares in the world and has twelve lines that cover the entire city. The Metro is open Monday – Friday (5 a.m. to midnight), Saturday (6 a.m.. to midnight), and Sunday (7 a.m. to midnight). The Metro is very crowded during the day and traveling during rush hours should be avoided. Tickets are sold at the ticket booth in each station. After passing through the turnstile, look for two large signs showing the destinations and follow the signs. Make sure you know where you are going as there is only one map with the routes at the entrance of the station. Note: SALIDA means EXIT and ANDENES means PLATFORMS. Once you get on the train, there's a map of the station stops for that line only located above each door. CORRESPONDENCIAS means transfer points. Be prepared to walk a bit inside the Metro system, especially when transferring lines. **Remember, this is not the safest way to travel and Metro pickpockets prey on tourists.**

Bus

Traveling by bus is common for locals. However, visitors should beware. There are bus stops on all the major tourist streets and most post a map with the full route description. The Metrobus, introduced in 2006, runs in its own designated lane up and down Avenida Insurgentes and usually travels faster than the surrounding traffic. Most of these buses are used by commuters but if you know where you're going and know the stop, the Metrobus is a better alternative to the other buses.

Microbuses

Some tourists like to use the peseros (microbuses); these are sedans or minibuses that run along major roadways. These buses have established fares and pick up and let off passengers along the route and usually offer a more comfortable ride and speedy journey. These microbuses are usually green and gray and display cards in the windshield with their routes. As the bus nears a stop, the driver will put his hand out the wind displaying one or more fingers indicating the number of passengers he can accommodate.

Tourist Bus

Many cities feature the red double-decker hop-on and hop-off tour buses (in Mexico City they are called **Turibuses; 55 5133 2488** or www.turibus.com.mx) and here in Mexico City they offer different tours in the north and south of the city. Each bus seats 75 and offers an audio tour in five languages. These buses operate from 9 a.m. to 9 p.m. and for a set fee tourists can hop-on and hop off as often as desired. One of their most popular tours is the Chapultepec-

Centro Histórico route with 25 stops including major monuments, museums and neighborhoods. Another favorite circuit takes passengers from La Roma neighborhood south with stops that include the World Trade Center, Plaza de Torros bullring, Carillo Gil museum, Perisur shopping center, and the Frida Kahlo museum. Another tour route goes to the pyramids at Teotihuacán.

Rental Car

If you are traveling without a car and want to travel to Puebla or other surrounding areas, you may consider a rental car. Be warned that due to the high percentage of auto theft, **renting a car in Mexico City is not recommended**.

Do not rent a car unless you're familiar with the area. These people drive like maniacs. The last thing you want is to be in a fender bender in this country where bribes are so common. If you're not prepared to deal with the police, avoid renting a car.

It is not advised to drive in the city if you're not familiar with the streets and neighborhoods, especially if you don't read Spanish, as all the signs are in Spanish, and you certainly don't want to take the chance of landing in one of the city's unsavory neighborhoods. One safe option is to hire a car with a driver—Avis offers chauffeur-driven rental cars at all of its Mexico City locations –the drivers know the area and are great tour guides. (Avis – 800-352-7900 in the U.S. or 1-800-288-8888 in Mexico).

A TO Z LISTINGS
Ridiculously Extravagant
Sensible Alternatives
Quality Bargain Spots

One good thing about eating in Mexico City is that it's possible to eat cheaply here from one end of town to the other. The street food is really terrific, maybe the best in the world except for certain cities in Southeast Asia. Every corner will have great food on it.

AZUL CONDESA
Nuevo León 68, Cuauhtémoc, Hipódromo, Mexico City, +52 55 5286 6268
www.azul.rest
CUISINE: Mexican
DRINKS: Full Bar
SERVING: Breakfast, Lunch
PRICE RANGE: $$$

NEIGHBORHOOD: Condesa
Chef Ricardo Munoz Zurita offers a menu of authentic Mexican cuisine in a simple atmosphere of wooden tables and chairs. Though the dining room is electric with activity, try to get one of the tables in the atrium garden if you can swing it. Very lush and tropical. Menu favorites include: Beef drizzled in a smoky Oaxacan mole, Veracruz style fish, and ancient Mayan dishes. Try the "enigmatico" chichilo negro, which is one of the 7 Oaxaca moles you seldom see. (It's made with chihuacle pepper ashes and is usually served with beef.)

AZUL HISTÓRICO
Isabel la Católica, 30, Centro Historico A, 52 55 5510 1316
www.azul.rest
CUISINE: Mexican
DRINKS: Full Bar
SERVING: Brunch, Lunch, Dinner
PRICE RANGE: $$$
NEIGHBORHOOD: Downtown south / Centro Sur
With lights in the thick-branched trees overhead, you couldn't find a more romantic spot than this popular restaurant serving favorites like Stuffed Duck Fritters dipped in mole and Black Chichilo Chiuacle Chili served with venison. This is also a great place for breakfast, serving favorites like chilaquiles, Mexican eggs, and enchiladas. Try the delicious house-made chocolate cake served with gorgonzola cheese ice cream.

BEATRICITA
Londres 190-D, Mexico City, 52 55 5511 4213
www.beatricita.com
CUISINE: Mexican street food
DRINKS: Beer & Wine
SERVING: Dinner
PRICE RANGE: $
NEIGHBORHOOD: Colonia Zona Rosa
If you're a fan of tacos, this is your place. Here in Coyoacán's main market you'll find a variety of great tacos and daily specials. One of the differences in the carnitas tacos you get in America and what you get here is that here they have cooked a whole pig, and you can choose if you want belly, leg, snout, whatever part of the pig you want. In America, it's usually just dry shredded pork, hardly the same.

BELMONDO
Tabasco 109, Mexico City, +55 62 73 2079
www.belmondo.com.mx/
CUISINE: Deli, Sandwiches
DRINKS: Wines
SERVING: Lunch & Dinner
PRICE RANGE: $
NEIGHBORHOOD: Roma Norte
This eatery draws lots of young creative and trendy types and offers a simple menu featuring salads, sandwiches as spot on and good as any you've had anywhere. Also a curated list of wines by the glass. Menu favorites include: the French dip with roast beef and gravy, or the grilled cheese with caramelized onions. Closed Sundays. Be prepared for a wait.

BÓSFORO
Luis Moya 31, Mexico City, +52 55 5512 1991
No Website
CUISINE: Mexican
DRINKS: Full Bar
SERVING: Breakfast, Lunch, Dinner

PRICE RANGE: $$
NEIGHBORHOOD: Federal District
This small friendly neighborhood bar specializes in mezcales and offers a menu of Mexican bar food with favorites like the quesadilla and tapas. Try the desserts especially if you're a chocolate lover.

CABRERA 7
Calle Plaza Luis Cabrera 7, Miguel Hidalgo, Mexico City, 52 55 5264 4531
CUISINE: Mexican
DRINKS: Full Bar
SERVING: Brunch, Lunch, Dinner
PRICE RANGE: $$
NEIGHBORHOOD: Roma Norte
This superb two-level restaurant and lounge bar (overlooking the gorgeous fountains decorating **Plaza Luis Cabrera**), and has a menu featuring Mexican

cuisine from all regions. Menu favorites include: Oaxacan mole, cochinita pibil, and of course the tacos and tortas. This place makes for great people-watching as artists set up makeshift stalls to sell their wares and the whole population flows by in a continuous and colorful parade of humanity.

CAFÉ EL POPULAR RESTAURANTE
5 de Mayo, No. 50-52, Mexico City, 52 55 5518-6081
No Website
CUISINE: Cafe
DRINKS: No Booze
SERVING: 24 hours
PRICE RANGE: $$
NEIGHBORHOOD: Central Historic District
This 24-hour café offers great Mexican breakfast like huevos rancheros or enchiladas verdes under a wood beamed ceiling. Great coffees and pastries. If you're lucky there will be live music.

CAFÉ NIN
Calle Havre 73, Juárez, Mexico, +52 55 5207 7065
www.cafenin.com.mx
CUISINE: Breakfast
DRINKS: No Booze
SERVING: Breakfast
PRICE RANGE: $$
NEIGHBORHOOD: Juárez
Great choice for breakfast and the most popular brunch spot in the area. Impressive selection of baked goods – everything from doughnuts to croissants and the best-ever guava cheese pastries. Delicious cappuccino. Nice small plates as well, like the avocado & squid ceviche.

CAFÉ PASSMAR Calle Adolfo Prieto s/n Local 237, Mexico City, +52 55 5669 1994
www.cafepassmar.com
CUISINE: Cafeteria/Coffeehouse
NEIGHBORHOOD: Benito Juárez
Just a coffeehouse that offers a full range of coffees beyond Starbucks presentation along with fruit smoothies, herbal teas, and frappes.

CHURRERIA EL MORO
Eje Central Lázaro Cárdenas 42, Col. Centro Histórico, Ciudad de México, +52 52 551 20896
www.elmoro.mx
CUISINE: Coffee shop
DRINKS: No Booze
SERVING: Open 24 hours
PRICE RANGE: $
NEIGHBORHOOD: Centro Sur
Churros, churros, churros. They have to be eaten when they're warm to be appreciated. Here at this bakery, where they do things the old-fashioned way, they make 'em to order, so you get fresh churros with a variety of toppings, everything from deep dark chocolate to dulce de leche.

CONTRAMAR
Calle de Durango 200, Mexico City, +52 55 5514 9217
www.contramar.com.mx
CUISINE: Seafood
DRINKS: Full Bar
SERVING: Lunch, Dinner
PRICE RANGE: $$$
NEIGHBORHOOD: Condesa

This seafood restaurant is considered one of the chicest dining halls in the whole country, and not so much for its food, which is fine, but for the eclectic mix of artists, hipsters and trendy types it attracts. Blue and white color scheme highlights the high-ceilinged room. Best people-watching in the city. Has a great selection of dishes, including Tuna Tostadas, Oysters & pescado a la talla, Crab Cakes, and Spaghetti with Clams.

COOX HANAL
Calle Isabel la Catolica 83, Centro Histórico, Centro, 06090 Ciudad de México, CDMX,
+52 55 5709 3613
www.cooxhanal.com
CUISINE: Mexican
DRINKS: Full bar
SERVING: Lunch & Dinner
PRICE RANGE: $$$
NEIGHBORHOOD: Central Historic District
Popular eatery (since 1953) on the second floor offering authentic Yucatan fare like *poc chuc* (pork grilled after being marinated in orange juice). Other menu picks: Chamorro and Lime soup. Live music. This place was originally opened by boxer Raul Salazar, from Yucatan's capital, Merida.

DELIRIO
Ave. Monterrey 116-b, Mexico City, +52 55 5584 0870
www.delirio.mx
CUISINE: French/Deli
DRINKS: Beer & Wine Only
SERVING: Breakfast, Lunch & Dinner; closed Mon

PRICE RANGE: $$
NEIGHBORHOOD: Roma Norte
Great place to stop if you're looking for non-Mexican fare. Light dishes like focaccia.

DULCE PATRIA
Anatole France 100, Mexico City, 52 55 3300 3999
www.dulcepatriamexico.com
CUISINE: Mexican
DRINKS: Full Bar
SERVING: Breakfast, Lunch
PRICE RANGE: $$$$
NEIGHBORHOOD: Polanco
Chef Martha Ortiz offers a menu of traditional Mexican cuisine with a modern twist. It's her innovative approach that has pushed her to the forefront of the "New Mexican" cuisine that's exploding all over the country (and abroad). This 90-seat eatery features two terraces inside the restaurant

giving an outdoor feel. Definitely begin with her ceviche. But also try her fabulous "sangritas" as a chaser after you down a shot of tequila.

EL CARDENAL
Palma 23, México, D.F., +52 55 5521 8815
www.restauranteelcardenal.com
CUISINE: Mexican
DRINKS: Full Bar
SERVING: Breakfast, Lunch, & Dinner
PRICE RANGE: $$
NEIGHBORHOOD: Centro Sur
Located in a beautiful old house, this popular eatery serves authentic Mexican fare. Favorites: Quesadillas with guac, and Chicken with nopales. Popular brunch spot. If you're there for one of the best breakfast in town, get the *huevos en caldo de frijol.*

EL FAROLITO
Altata 19, Col. Condesa, México, D.F., +52 55 5273 7297
www.taqueriaselfarolito.com.mx
CUISINE: Tacos
DRINKS: No Booze
SERVING: Lunch & Dinner
PRICE RANGE: $
NEIGHBORHOOD: Condesa
Delicious Mexican fare prepared right in front of you at this decades-old spot with several locations. Try the Faroladas de Bisteck (Pita bread with steak and cheese). Nice selection of fruit juices.

EL HIDALGUENSE

Campeche 155, Mexico City, +52 55 5564 0538
No Website
CUISINE: Mexican
DRINKS: No Booze
SERVING: Open only 7 a.m. – 5 p.m. Fri - Sun
PRICE RANGE: $$
NEIGHBORHOOD: Roma Sur
A locals' favorite, this Mexican eatery offers a great selection of barbecue, meats, montalayo, and seafood. Authentic Mexican fare.

EL MAYOR

República de Argentina 15, Col. Centro, Mexico City, 52 55 5704 7580
www.restaurantelmayor.com.mx
CUISINE: Mexican
DRINKS: Full Bar
SERVING: Brunch, Lunch
PRICE RANGE: $$
NEIGHBORHOOD: Centro Histórico
Located on the top floor above a bookstore, this modern restaurant offers a menu of Mexican favorites and European-influenced fusion dishes. This is also a great place for brunch. There's a rooftop bar that overlooks the ruins of the Aztec city.

EL TURIX
Emilio Castelar, 212, Mexico City, 52 55 5280 6449
CUISINE: Mexican
DRINKS: Beer & Wine
SERVING: Lunch, Dinner
PRICE RANGE: $
NEIGHBORHOOD: Colonia Polanco
Located in a dingy storefront, but the food is worth the visit. There's an outdoor patio and a couple tables inside. Menu favorites include Cochinita pibil (pork slowly cooked with achiote that is a specialty of the Yucatán) and Tamales.

EL VENADITO
Universidad 1701, Col. Chimalistac, México, D.F., +52 55 5661 9786
No Web Site
CUISINE: Tacos
DRINKS: Beer & Wine
SERVING: Lunch & Dinner
PRICE RANGE: $
NEIGHBORHOOD: Florida
For over 50 years this place has served typical Mexican fare to lines of happy customers. Known for their great Carnitas. Favorites: Enchiladas, tacos al pastor and French toast dessert. Across the street you can see the Chapel of San Jose del Atillo.

ENO
Francisco Petrarca 258, Mexico City, +52 55 5531 8300
www.eno.com.mx
CUISINE: Sandwiches
DRINKS: Beer & Wine Only
SERVING: Breakfast, Lunch & Dinner
PRICE RANGE: $$
NEIGHBORHOOD: Polanco
Casual eatery that specializes in sandwiches. Great spot for breakfast or lunch. Seating is communal. Favorites include the carnitas de atun (seared tuna) sandwich.

FLOR DE LIS

Avenida Mazatlan 30, Condesa, Mexico City, 52 55 5211 0060
www.tamalesyatole.com
CUISINE: Mexican
DRINKS: Beer & Wine
SERVING: Dinner
PRICE RANGE: $
NEIGHBORHOOD: Condesa
If you're looking for tamales, this is your place. There's a nice variety including chicken, peppers, beef, mole, and sweet (fruit). The atmosphere is quaint but the food is solid. Menu favorites included the Chicken and tomato tamale wrapped in banana leaf.

FONDA MARGARITA

Adolfo Prieto 1364, Mexico City, +52 55 5559 6358
CUISINE: Mexican
DRINKS: No Booze
SERVING: Breakfast, Lunch & Dinner
PRICE RANGE: $
NEIGHBORHOOD: Benito Juarez
Authentic Mexican cuisine typical of the region. Try the chicharrones in green sauce served with fresh tortillas and eggs and beans. Very few vegetarian options. Spanish speaking only.

FONDA MAYORA
Campeche 322, Hipódromo, Mexico City, +52 55 6843 0595
CUISINE: Mexican
DRINKS: Full bar
SERVING: Breakfast, Lunch & Dinner (early)
PRICE RANGE: $$$
NEIGHBORHOOD: Condesa
Chef Gerardo Vázquez Lugo offers a menu of traditional Mexican fare. The best was the guacamole served from a cart and mixed to order with your choice of onions, tomatoes, and avocado. Everything is served fresh. Not a tourist destination.

HAVRE 77
Havre 77, Col. Juárez, México, D.F., 5208 1070
No Website
CUISINE: French-Mexican
DRINKS: No Booze
SERVING: Breakfast, Lunch; closed Mon & Tues
PRICE RANGE: $$$$
NEIGHBORHOOD: Juárez

Small eatery reminiscent of cafes in Paris. A perfect place to stop when you want a break from Mexican food. Favorites: Steak frites, Escargots du Jour and Laitue (salad with fresh tarragon). Delicious French pastries make this a nice stop early in the morning.

HOSTERIA DE SANTO DOMINGO
Calle Belisario Dominguez 72, 06010 México, D.F., +52 55 5526 5276
No Website
CUISINE: Mexican
DRINKS: Full bar
SERVING: Breakfast, Lunch & Dinner
PRICE RANGE: $$
NEIGHBORHOOD: Centro Norte
Traditional authentic Mexican fare in the city's oldest restaurant that opened in the 1860s. Gourmet dishes featuring meats and fish, like the *chile en nogado*, large poblano chile peppers stuffed full of ground meat, dried fruit and topped with a rich, creamy sauce. Live music. The atmosphere may remind you of your grandmother's house, or, come to think of it, your great-grandmother's house.

GUZINA OAXACA
Masaryk 513, Mexico City**, +52 55 5282 1820**
www.guzinaoaxaca.com
CUISINE: Mexican
DRINKS: Full bar
SERVING: Breakfast, Lunch & Dinner
PRICE RANGE: $$
NEIGHBORHOOD: Polanco
Chef Alejandro Ruíz recently opened this location of his acclaimed Oaxaca eatery serving contemporary

Mexican fare. Here you'll get delicious homemade tortillas, tableside served Oaxacan salsa, and mole. Great choice for breakfast. Make reservations for this place.

LA BARRACA VALENCIANA
Centenario 91-C, Col. Del Carmen, Mexico City, +52 55 5658 1880
www.labarracavalenciana.com
CUISINE: Spanish/Tapas/Small Plates
DRINKS: Beer & Wine Only
SERVING: Lunch & Dinner; closed Sun
PRICE RANGE: $$
NEIGHBORHOOD: Coyoacán
Small eatery (only 12 tables) serving a menu of tapas and small plates. Favorites include: Squid Roman, Grilled chicken breast and Chamorro veal. Specials change weekly.

LA CASA DE LAS SIRENAS
República de Guatemala 32, Mexico City, 52 55 5704 3345
www.lacasadelassirenas.com.mx
CUISINE: Continental
DRINKS: Full Bar
SERVING: Breakfast, Lunch, Dinner
PRICE RANGE: $$$
NEIGHBORHOOD: Centro Histórico (Central Historic)
This charming restaurant overlooks the Cathedral of Mexico City and the National Palace. Menu favorites

include: Roast chicken and Rib Eye. Delicious desserts. The restaurant features a tequila salon with dozens of agave spirits and a rooftop with tables that look into the cathedral's garden.

LA CASTELLANA
AV Revolucion 1309 esq Corregidora, Mexico City, 52 55 5593 4916
www.tortaslacastellana.com
CUISINE: Mexican
DRINKS: Beer & Wine
SERVING: Lunch, Dinner
PRICE RANGE: $
Specializing in tortas, this is just one of five locations. The tortas are made with crisp-crusted and light bread, pickled jalapenos and a variety of fillings. And cheap, cheap, cheap.

LA DOCENA OYSTER BAR
Av. Álvaro Obregón 31, Mexico City, +52 55 5208 0748
www.ladocena.com.mx
CUISINE: Seafood
DRINKS: Full bar
SERVING: Lunch & Dinner
PRICE RANGE: $$$
NEIGHBORHOOD: Roma Norte
Seafood eatery specializing in oysters and barbecue. Favorite dish: Baby squid with garlic. Creative selection of desserts. Reservations recommended. English menu available.

LALO!
Calle Zacatecas 173, Mexico City, +52 55 5564 3388
www.eat-lalo.com
CUISINE: Breakfast/Pizza
DRINKS: Beer & Wine Only

SERVING: Breakfast, Lunch & Dinner; Lunch only on Mon
PRICE RANGE: $$
NEIGHBORHOOD: Roma Norte
Chef Eduardo Garcia's casual eatery just across the street from his more upscale eatery Maximo Bistrot. Great choice for breakfast – have the French toast. Amazing selection of pastries and house-made yogurt. Dinner choices include dishes like freshly made octopus with arugula.

LARDO
Agustín Melgar 6, Cuauhtemoc, Mexico City, +52 55 5211 7731
www.lardo.mx
CUISINE: French
DRINKS: Full bar
SERVING: Lunch & Dinner
PRICE RANGE: $$
NEIGHBORHOOD: Condesa
Hip eatery with a menu of Mexican and international cuisine. Great selection of seafood and seasonal dishes. They will even make dishes to order. Nice selection of wines.

LAS CAZUELAS DE LA ABUELA
Av San Jeronimo 630, Mexico City, +52 55 5683 8720
https://las-cazuelas-de-la-abuela.business.site
CUISINE: Mexican
DRINKS: Full Bar
SERVING: Dinner
PRICE RANGE: $
NEIGHBORHOOD: Pedregal

This family restaurant offers a menu of Mexican cuisine with Poblano overtones. The menu features 25 different stews and delicious peneques – a deep-fried quesadilla with green and red pumpkin-seed sauce.

LOS PANCHOS
Calle Tolstoi 9, Miguel Hidalgo, +52 55 5254 5390
www.lospanchos.mx
CUISINE: Mexican
DRINKS: Full bar
SERVING: Breakfast, Lunch & Dinner
PRICE RANGE: $$
NEIGHBORHOOD: Anzures
Great place for a family dinner.
Traditional Mexican eatery that's worth a try. Great dishes and the steak here is exceptional (not your typical American steak). Nice selection of desserts.

MAISON ARTEMISIA
Tonalá 23, Cuauhtémoc, Mexico City, +52 55 6303 2471
www.maisonartemisia.com
CUISINE: French
DRINKS: Full bar
SERVING: Lunch & Dinner; closed Sun
PRICE RANGE: $$$
NEIGHBORHOOD: Roma Norte
Upscale dining with an upstairs piano bar. Restaurant offers a nice selection of seafood and beef. Favorites include: Grilled octopus and Short-rib ravioli.
This place is famous for its imported absinthe and absinthe-based cocktails.

MAXIMO BISTROT LOCAL
Tonalá 133, Mexico City, 52 55 5264 4291
www.maximobistrot.com.mx
CUISINE: Mexican, Italian, French
DRINKS: Wine
SERVING: Lunch, Dinner
PRICE RANGE: $$$$
NEIGHBORHOOD: Roma Norte
This rustic bistro, run by a young husband-and-wife team, offers a daily menu featuring ingredients found in the local markets. It has an open kitchen and has handwritten daily menus. Menu favorites include: Lamb loin and Tartar of Steelhead. Reservations required.

MERCADO ROMA COYOACAN
Miguel Angel Quevedo 353, Mexicto DF, 55 2155 9435
www.mrc.mercadoroma.com
NEIGHBORHOOD: Coyoacán
Over 40 wildly diverse vendors occupy the 3 floors of this spectacular market, and a lot of them are eateries offering up authentic Mexican fare. While this is basically a collection of upscale food vendors that replicate the down-and-dirty street food you can find all over the city, in this place things are a little tidier, and the excitement stems from the fact that you can sample Mexican-fusion this or that, getting tastes from the far corners of this country. You can get tacos from 9 different regions of the country. But also elements of cuisine from around the world, all blended into Mexicsn cuisince. An Italian vendor serves tacos, but the taco is *piadina*, which is like a tortilla, but comes from Italy. Hundreds of surprising (and pleasing)

combinations like this will enchant you. If you're on a short visit, this place ought to be a must, because you'll get to experience so much so fast.

MERENDERO LAS LUPITAS
Plaza Santa Catarina 4, Col. Del Carmen, México, D.F., +52 55 5554 3353
www.merenderolaslupitas.com.mx/
CUISINE: Mexican
DRINKS: No Booze
SERVING: Breakfast, Lunch; closed Mon & Tues
PRICE RANGE: $$
NEIGHBORHOOD: Coyoacán
Family-run eatery offering authentic Northern Mexican fare. Try the atole (a corn based drink served hot). Favorites: Chimichangas, egg & bean dishes and Flan.

MERO TORO
Calle Amsterdam 204, Mexico City, +52 55 5564 7799
www.merotoro.mx
CUISINE: Northern Mexican
DRINKS: Full Bar
SERVING: Dinner
PRICE RANGE: $$$
NEIGHBORHOOD: Condesa
Open since 2010, this eatery brings the surf-and-turf cuisine of Baja California to the Mexican highlands. Chef Jair Tellez created the expansive menu. Selections start with the small plate men featuring dishes like Ceviche ligero but don't forget the delicious main courses like Gently roasted grouper served on a bed of puréed cauliflower.

MOG
Frontera 168, Col. Roma, 52 55 5264 1629
No Website
CUISINE: Asian
DRINKS: Beer & Wine Only
SERVING: Lunch, Dinner
PRICE RANGE: $$
NEIGHBORHOOD: Roma Norte

This popular eatery offers a menu of sushi, Japanese style dishes and fusion. The bar serves a variety of Mexican and Japanese beers and sakes. Menu favorites include: Sushi rolls, Teriyaki Chicken and Yakimeshi. Desserts favorites include the green tea cake.

PAPRIKA
Masella 61, Col. Juarez, Mexico City, +52 55 5533 0303
CUISINE: Mediterranean/Moroccan/Arabian
DRINKS: Full bar
SERVING: Lunch & Dinner; closed Sun
PRICE RANGE: $$
NEIGHBORHOOD: Juárez
Middle eastern eatery with a menu of small plate dishes created by Chef Josefina Santacruz. Popular dishes like Lamb and lentils served with rice, pistachios and apricots. Nice menu of teas.

PASTELERIA LA GRAN VIA
Amsterdan 288-A, Mexico City, +52 55 5574 4008
www.pastelerialagranvia.com
CUISINE: Bakery/Specialty Grocery
NEIGHBORHOOD: Condesa
Popular bakery featuring a variety of breads, pastries, doughnuts, cakes and cookies. Great meringues and low-sugar options.

PUJOL

Tennyson 133, Mexico City, 52 55 5545 4111
www.pujol.com.mx
CUISINE: Mexican/Fusion
DRINKS: Full Bar
SERVING: Brunch, Lunch, Dinner
PRICE RANGE: $$$$
NEIGHBORHOOD: Polanco

With a reputation as one of the world's best restaurants (and hardest to get into with only a baker's dozen tables), this Mexican eatery mixes modern (mostly French-inspired) and ancient culinary techniques. Prix-fix menu. Menu favorites include: Fish ceviche taco and Fried pork belly. As an example of Chef Enrique Olvera's innovative culinary talents, I ordered tacos that had baby lamb, avocado-pera purée and the pungently aromatic herb, *hoja santa*. Delicious. This is why Olvera is Mexico's most famous chef.

QUINTONIL
Newton 55, Mexico City, +52 55 5280 1660
www.quintonil.com
CUISINE: Mexican
DRINKS: Full Bar
SERVING: Dinner
PRICE RANGE: $$$
NEIGHBORHOOD: Polanaco
This place takes traditional Mexican cuisine to the next level. Great margaritas and Mexican wines. Menu favorites include: Swiss chard tamale with raison puree; delicate slices of *chilacayote* squash and charred tortillas are topped with mole; *Huauzontle*, which is something similar to broccoli, is fried and served with salsa and cheese from Chiapas.

RESTAURANTE BAR CHON
Regina 160, 06090 México, D.F. +52 55 5542 0873
CUISINE: Mexican; Pre-Hispanic cuisine as well
DRINKS: Full bar

SERVING: Lunch & Dinner; closed Sunday
PRICE RANGE: $$$
NEIGHBORHOOD: Centro Sur

Traditional Mexican fare with most entrees based around the tortilla, rice and beans. This is one of the few places that also serves Pre-Hispanic food, so you can see what it was like to eat before Europeans arrived to muck it all up for the Indians. Unique offerings featuring insects, grasshoppers, worms, ant larvae and wild boar. Try the *pulque* ("blood of the gods"), a flavored beverage. A once-in-a-lifetime experience.

ROKAI

Rio Ebro 87, Mexico City, 55 5207 7543
http://edokobayashi.com/index.php/rokai/
CUISINE: Japanese
DRINKS: Beer, Wine & Sake
SERVING: Lunch, Dinner; closed Sunday
PRICE RANGE: $
NEIGHBORHOOD: Cuauhtémoc

A favorite among locals and foodies, this small

Japanese eatery serves up famous dishes like Rokai, mussels sake, tuna, rib eye and duck, red snapper with Himalayan salt and yuzu paste and Ensenada Octopus sashimi. They also have a menu with nine or ten courses –changing daily. They also have a real standout menu item in their fried chicken. What makes it different (and a delightful surprise for a South Carolina boy like myself) is that it's marinated in sake. The bar offers hot sake, green tea, Sapporo beer and wine.

ROMITA COMEDOR
Álvaro Obregón 49, Mexico City, 55 5525 8975
www.romitacomedor.com
CUISINE: Mexican
DRINKS: Full Bar
SERVING: Dinner

PRICE RANGE: $$
NEIGHBORHOOD: Roma Norte
They have a casual ambiance here on the top 2 floors of a mansion from the early part of the 20th Century that now looks like a reinvented greenhouse. The floors are checkerboard and there's a glass roof that retracts in good weather. Though the food is good, it's the place itself that's the main attraction. This place is so popular it often takes weeks to get a reservation. They serve up a traditional Mexican menu: Octopus; Ribs; or try the taco del río (with langoustines in a tomato-and-morita-chile sauce). Great cocktails and they also serve a house blend Sangria.

SUD777
Blvd. de la Luz 777, Col. Jardines del Pedregal, México, D.F., +52 55 5568 4777
www.sud777.com.mx/web2
CUISINE: Mexican
DRINKS: Full Bar
SERVING: Breakfast, Lunch, & Dinner
PRICE RANGE: $$$
NEIGHBORHOOD: Jardines del Pedregal
Great dining experience in a classic restaurant open since 2008 that offers cutting edge innovative cuisine while relying on traditional Mexican ingredients. Updated, modern, but still somehow traditional. The crisscrossing beams above give the place a modern look, as vines weave in and out of nooks and crannies. Light brown wooden tables mix with the blacks and grays to highlight the intimate décor. The chef swears he never uses any produce that's not Mexican. (I believe him.) There is a tasting menu, which I highly recommend. Be sure to get the wine pairing, because

this place has one of the best selections of really local Mexican wines to be had in the city. Too many other upscale restaurants focus on foreign labels. Favorites: Tuna tostada with soy, Lechon pork, poblano chiles, Cotija cheese, a foie gras that's made locally and Crab ceviche. (There also a super good sushi bar, **Kokeshi**, tucked away inside this place.)

TABERNA DEL LEON
Altamirano 46, Col.Tizapán San Ángel, 01000 México, D.F., +52 55 5616 2110
www.latabernadelleon.com.mx
CUISINE: Mexican gourmet
DRINKS: Full bar
SERVING: Lunch & Dinner
PRICE RANGE: $$$$
NEIGHBORHOOD: San Angel
Beautiful upscale though casual eatery offering an exceptional dining experience. Favorites: Pork chop with Brussel sprouts and Foie gras; *robalo a los tres chiles* (bass cooked with a three-pepper chili sauce). Excellent desserts like Chocolate cake served with raspberry ice cream.

TACOS MANOLO
Luz Saviñón 1305 (bet. Anaxágoras and Cauhtémoc), Mexico City, 52 55 4437 1463
No Website
CUISINE: Mexican
DRINKS:
SERVING: Lunch, Dinner
PRICE RANGE: $$
NEIGHBORHOOD: Colonia Del Valle
This busy stand is all about tacos. Try the classic Manolo, chopped bistec with onion and bacon.

TAQUERIA EL CALIFA
Altata 22, Mexico City, +52 55 5271 7666
www.elcalifa.com.mx/web/
CUISINE: Mexican
DRINKS: Beer & Wine
SERVING: Dinner
PRICE RANGE: $$
NEIGHBORHOOD: Condesa
A popular taqueria with traditional favorites like the chicharon de queso and the Gaona conqueso.

TAQUERIA EL PROGRESO
Calle Maestro Antonio Caso 30, Col. Tabacalera, +52 55 5546 4700
https://taqueriaelprogreso.negocio.site/
CUISINE: Tacos
DRINKS: No Booze
SERVING: Breakfast, Lunch; closed Mon & Tues
PRICE RANGE: $
NEIGHBORHOOD: Tabacalera
Tacos at this great little sidewalk café are served with a variety of meats and lots of toppings including mashed potatoes, beans, cactus, manzanita peppers and onions. Cow head tacos served here (tacos de cabeza), as well as the excellent cow brain. (Check out the juice bar next door.)

TAQUERIA LOS COCUYOS
Calle Bolívar 56, Mexico City, 52 55 5518 4231
No Website
CUISINE: Tacos
DRINKS: Full Bar

SERVING: Lunch, Dinner
PRICE RANGE: $
NEIGHBORHOOD: Centro
This little taqueria offers up an interesting menu of tacos. Menu favorites include: Suadero (braised and seared beef) and Beef tongue taco.

TETETLAN
Av. de Las Fuentes 180, Col. Jardines del Pedregal, Ciudad de México, +52 55 5668 5335
www.tetetlan.com
CUISINE: Mexican
DRINKS: Full Bar
SERVING: Breakfast, Lunch, & Dinner
PRICE RANGE: $$
NEIGHBORHOOD: Pedregal
Located off the beaten path is this ultra-trendy eatery, that uses many different kinds of stone in its walls, rocks, bricks, poured concrete. Lots of weird angles, nooks and crannies. Completely charming. The name of this place actually means "place of many stones." You'll love it. They offer a menu of international and regional cuisine, boasting that over 90% of what they use comes from Mexico. Favorites: Roasted huitlacoche (this is a fungus that grows on corn), dried crickets with lemon and Tamales with hoja santa. Nice selection of tequilas.

TORTAS EL CAPRICHO
Augusto Rodin, 407, Mexico City, 52 55 3330 3935
CUISINE: Mexican
DRINKS: Beer & Wine
SERVING: Lunch, Dinner
PRICE RANGE: $
NEIGHBORHOOD: Colonia Mixoac
This eatery, very popular among the locals, specializes in tortas, large cake sandwiches, and offers nearly 50 varieties.

YUBAN
Colima 268, Mexico City, 52 55 6387 0358
www.yuban.mx
CUISINE: Mexican
DRINKS: Full Bar
SERVING: Lunch, Dinner
PRICE RANGE: $
NEIGHBORHOOD: Roma Norte
Chef Paloma Ortiz offers a menu featuring a variety of traditional recipes with a contemporary flair. There's a big emphasis on the *moles* from Oaxaca Sierre Norte region. Menu favorites include: Smoky chichilo and the classic tlayuda. Desserts include a multi-dimensional multi-layer chocolate cake made with Oaxacan chocolate. At night the place becomes a hip hangout.

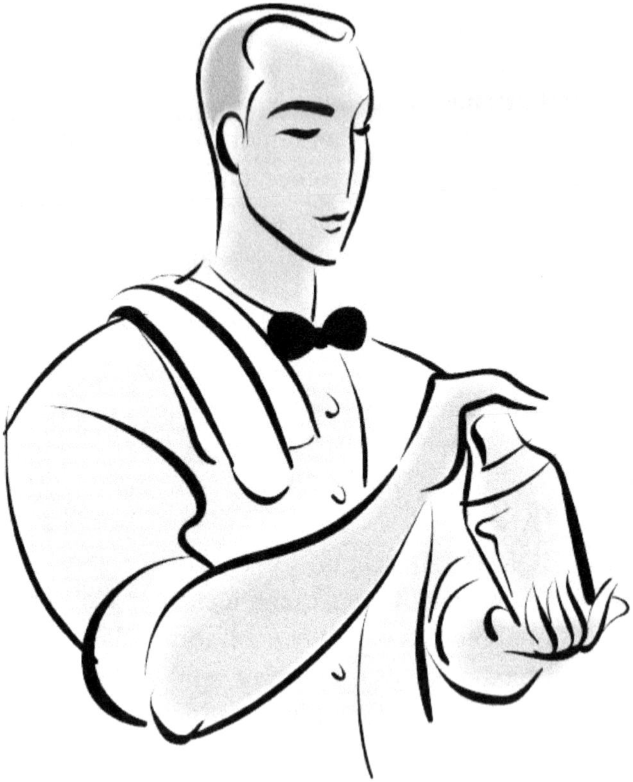

NIGHTLIFE

EL DEPÓSITO
Álvaro Obregón 21, Local 1, Mexico City, 52-55-5207-8152
www.eldeposito.com.mx
NEIGHBORHOOD: Condesa
This is part of a small chain of beer-bar-bottle shops that offer a wide selection of over 160 beers. Here you'll find a great selection of beer on tap, Mexican micros, European imports, German beers and a few Belgians. There's a terrace, TV, and free popcorn.

EL REAL UNDER
Monterey 80, Col. Roma, 52 55 5511 5475
http://theunder.org/real/
NEIGHBORHOOD: Condesa
Another happening dance club.

FIFTY MILS
Paseo de la Reforma 500, Col. Juárez, México, D.F., +52 55 5230 1806
www.fiftymils.com
NEIGHBORHOOD: Juárez
Amazing quaint bar located in the **Four Seasons Hotel**. The Manhattan is their signature cocktail and it's top-notch. The bartenders are pros. But look closely at the "Creations" cocktail menu, which has cocktails unique to this wonderful lounge. Like Ant Man, which uses mescal, ants, egg whites, avocado, hoja santa bitters, soda water & lemongrass syrup. And that's just one cocktail! Plenty more to keep you busy. Hungry? Try the bar snacks like Grilled octopus with pineapple. Since you're here at the Four Seasons, try out the main restaurant, **IL BECCO**, featuring superior cuisine from the Piedmont region and a wondrous Italian wine list that will raise an eyebrow or two.

PULQUERIA LA HERMOSA HORTENSIA
Callejón de la Amargura 4, Plaza Garibaldi 4, 52-55-5529 7316
No Website
NEIGHBORHOOD: Centro Norte
Located on the far corner of the Plaza Garibaldi, this pulquería is a must-stop for visitors. It's a 77-year old pulque bar that serves the lightly alcoholic Aztec drink, made from the maguey plant. The drink has the color of milk and comes in flavors like strawberry and coconut. This bar is included in the Museos Vivos project (which highlights "Living Museums"- every day venues that have cultural and historic significance).

M.N. ROY
Mérida 186, San Luis Potosi
NEIGHBORHGOOD: Roma
www.mnroyclub.com

Emmanuel Picault opened this club and named it after the Indian revolutionary and founder of the Communist parties in both Mexico and India. It's super cool and gorgeously designed. Had throbbing house music late into the night. Dress to impress. It's a slick crowd here, even though the outside is designed to look like a simple ice cream parlor with a door the color of pink carnations.

PATRICK MILLER
Mérida 17, Mexico City, 52 55 5511 5406
www.patrickmiller.com.mx
WEBSITE DOWN AT PRESSTIME
NEIGHBORHOOD: Roma Norte
This is an old school disco featuring high-energy '80s dance music, laser lights and neon graffiti. Named after a popular DJ, this club opened during the Gloria Gayner golden days of disco and has been running strong ever since. The eclectic crowd is filled with flashy dressers, flamboyant transvestites, and disco divas. No hard liquor here, just beer.

RHODESIA CLUB SOCIAL
Durango, 181, 52 55 5533 8208
www.clubsocialrhodesia.tv
NEIGHBORHGOOD: Roma

INDEX

Symbols

\
 Spanish, **36**
PULQUERIA LA HERMOSA HORTENSIA, **59**

A

Arabian, **45**
AZUL CONDESA, **20**
AZUL HISTÓRICO, **21**

B

BEATRICITA, **22**
BELMONDO, **23**
BÓSFORO, **23**
Breakfast, **38**
Bus, **15**

C

CABRERA 7, **24**
CAFÉ EL POPULAR RESTAURANTE, **25**
CAFÉ NIN, **25**
CHON, **47**
CHURRERIA EL MORO, **26**
CONTRAMAR, **26**
COOX HANAL, **27**

D

Deli, **27**
DELIRIO, **27**
DULCE PATRIA, **28**

E

EL CARDENAL, **29**
EL DEPÓSITO, **57**
EL FAROLITO, **29**
EL HIDALGUENSE, **30**
EL MAYOR, **30**
EL REAL UNDER, **58**
EL TURIX, **31**
EL VENADITO, **32**
ENO, **32**

F

FIFTY MILS, **58**
FLOR DE LIS, **33**
FONDA MARGARITA, **33**
FONDA MAYORA, **34**
Four Seasons Hotel, **58**
French, **27**, **39**, **40**

G

GUZINA OAXACA, **35**

H

HAVRE 77, **34**
HOSTERIA DE SANTO DOMINGO, **35**

I

IL BECCO, **58**

K

Kokeshi, **51**

L

LA BARRACA VALENCIANA, **36**
LA CASA DE LAS SIRENAS, **36**
LA CASTELLANA, **37**
LA DOCENA OYSTER BAR, **38**

LALO!, 38
LARDO, 39
LAS CAZUELAS DE LA ABUELA, 39
LOS PANCHOS, 40

M

MAISON ARTEMISIA, 40
MAXIMO BISTROT LOCAL, 41
Mediterranean, 45
MERCADO ROMA COYOACAN, 41
MERENDERO LAS LUPITAS, 42
MERO TORO, 43
Metered Taxis, 13
Metro, 14
Mexican, 27, 30, 33, 34, 35, 40, 47, 51
Microbuses, 16
M.N. ROY, 60
MOG, 44
Moroccan, 45

P

PAPRIKA, 45
PASTELERIA LA GRAN VIA, 45
PATRICK MILLER, 61
Peruvian, 26, 45
Pizza, 38
Plaza Luis Cabrera, 24
PUJOL, 46

Q

QUINTONIL, 47

R

Rental Car, 17
RESTAURANTE BAR CHON, 47
RHODESIA CLUB SOCIAL, 62
ROKAI, 48
ROMITA COMEDOR, 49

S

Sandwiches, **32**
Seafood, **38**
SUD777, **50**

T

TABERNA DEL LEON, **51**
TACOS MANOLO, **52**
Tapas/Small Plates, **36**
TAQUERIA EL CALIFA, **52**
TAQUERIA EL PROGRESO, **53**
TAQUERIA LOS COCUYOS, **53**
TETETLAN, **54**
TORTAS EL CAPRICHO, **55**
Tourist Bus, **16**
Turismo\, **12**

Y

YUBAN, **55**

Other Books by the Same Author

Andrew Delaplaine has written in widely varied fields: screenplays, novels (adult and juvenile), travel writing, journalism. His books are available in quality bookstores as well as all online retailers.

JACK HOUSTON / ST. CLAIR POLITICAL THRILLERS

THE KEYSTONE FILE – PART 1
THE KEYSTONE FILE – PART 2
THE KEYSTONE FILE – PART 3
THE KEYSTONE FILE – PART 4
THE KEYSTONE FILE – PART 5
THE KEYSTONE FILE – PART 6
THE KEYSTONE FILE – PART 7 *(FINAL)*

On Election night, as China and Russia mass soldiers on their common border in preparation for war, there's a tie in the Electoral College that forces the decision for President into the House of Representatives as mandated by the Constitution. The incumbent Republican President, working through his Aide for Congressional Liaison, uses the Keystone File, which contains dirt on every member of Congress, to blackmail members into supporting the Republican candidate. The action runs from Election Night in November to Inauguration Day on January 20. Jack Houston St. Clair runs a small detective agency in Miami. His father is Florida Governor Sam Houston St. Clair, the Republican candidate. While he tries to help his dad win the election, Jack also gets hired to follow up on some suspicious wire transfers involving drug smugglers, leading him to a sunken narco-sub off Key West that has $65 million in cash in its hull.

THE RUNNING MATE

Sam Houston St. Clair has been President for four long years and right now he's bogged down in a nasty fight to be re-elected. A Secret Service agent protecting the opposing candidate discovers that the candidate is sleeping with someone he shouldn't be, and tells his lifelong friend, the President's son Jack, this vital information so Jack can pass it on to help his father win the election. The candidate's wife has also found out about the clandestine affair and plots to kill the lover if her husband wins the election. Jack goes to Washington, and becomes involved in an international whirlpool of intrigue.

AFTER THE OATH: DAY ONE
AFTER THE OATH: MARCH WINDS
WEDDING AT THE WHITE HOUSE

Only three months have passed since Sam Houston St. Clair was sworn in as the new President, but a lot has happened. Returning from Vienna where he met with Russian and Chinese diplomats, Sam is making his way back to Flagler Hall in Miami, his first trip home since being inaugurated. Son Jack is in the midst of turmoil of his own back in Miami, dealing with various dramas, not the least of which is his increasing alienation from Babylon Fuentes and his growing attraction to the seductive Lupe Rodriguez. Fernando Pozo addresses new problems as he struggles to expand Cuba's secret operations in the U.S., made even more difficult as U.S.-Cuban relations thaw. As his father returns home, Jack knows Sam will find as much trouble at home as he did in Vienna.

THE ADVENTURES OF SHERLOCK HOLMES IV

In this series, the original Sherlock Holmes's great-great-great grandson solves crimes and mysteries in the present day, working out of the boutique hotel he owns on South Beach.

THE OKEECHOBEE MURDER

Sherlock Holmes and Watson are called to a remote area of Florida overlooking Lake Okeechobee to investigate a murder where all the evidence points to the victim's son as the killer. Holmes, however, is not so sure.

A MYSTERY IN KEY WEST

Holmes's doctor orders him to take a short holiday in Key West, and while there, Holmes is called on to look into a case in which three people involved in a Santería ritual died with no explanation.

THE CLEVER ONE

A former nun who, while still very devout, has renounced her vows so that she could "find a life, and possibly love, in the real world." She comes to Holmes in hopes that he can find out what happened to the man who promised to marry her, but mysteriously disappeared moments before their wedding.

ENIGMA IN THE REDLANDS

A nanny reaches out to Sherlock Holmes seeking his advice on whether she should take a new position when her prospective employer has demanded that she cut her hair as part of the job.

MEXICO CITY   69

THE RED-HAIRED MAN
A man with a shock of red hair calls on Sherlock Holmes to solve the mystery of the Red-haired League.

TOO MANY NAPOLEONS
Inspector Lestrade calls on Holmes to help him figure out why a madman would go around Miami breaking into homes and businesses to destroy cheap busts of the French Emperor. It all seems very insignificant to Holmes—until, of course, a murder occurs.

THE MISSING MAN IN THE WINDOW
In what seems to be the case of a missing person, Sherlock Holmes navigates his way through a maze of perplexing clues that leads him through a sinister world to a surprising conclusion.

THE BORNHOLM DIAMOND
A mysterious Swedish nobleman requests a meeting to discuss a matter of such serious importance that it may threaten the line of succession in one of the oldest royal houses in Europe.

SEVERAL TITLES IN THE DELAPLAINE SERIES OF PRE-SCHOOL READERS FOR CHILDREN

THE DELAPLAINE LONG WEEKEND TRAVEL GUIDE SERIES

Delaplaine Travel Guides represent the author's take on some of the many cities he's visited and many of which he has called home (for months or even years) during a lifetime of travel. The books are available as either ebooks or as printed books. Owing to the ease with which material can be uploaded, both the printed and ebook editions are updated 3 times a year.

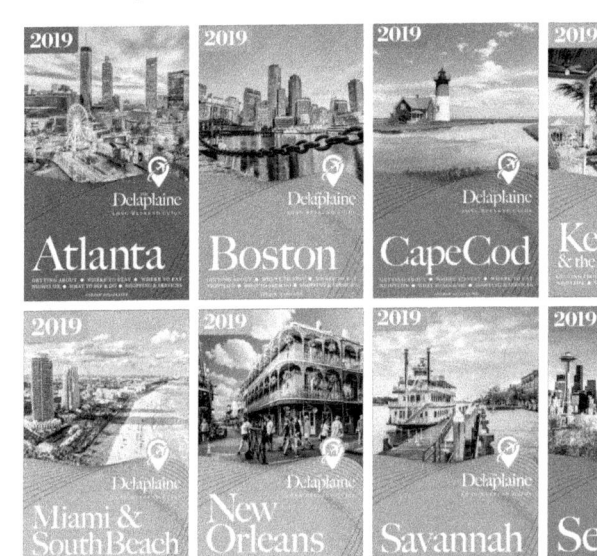

Atlanta
Austin
Boston
Cancún (Mexico)
Cannes
Cape Cod
Charleston
Chicago
Clearwater – St. Petersburg
Fort Lauderdale
Fort Myers & Sanibel

Gettysburg
Hamptons, The
Key West & the Florida Keys
Las Vegas
Louisville
Marseille
Martha's Vineyard
Memphis
Mérida (Mexico)
Mexico City
Miami & South Beach

Milwaukee
Myrtle Beach
Nantucket
Napa Valley
Naples & Marco Island
Nashville
New Orleans
Newport (R.I.)
Philadelphia
Provincetown
Savannah
Seattle

THE FOOD ENTHUSIAST'S COMPLETE RESTAURANT GUIDES

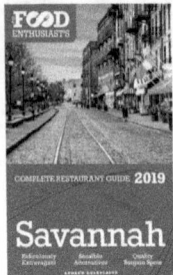

Atlanta
Austin
Barcelona
Boston
Brooklyn
Buenos Aires
Cannes
Cape Cod
Charleston
Chicago
Florence
Fort Lauderdale
Fort Myers & Sanibel
Gettysburg
Hampton, The

Key West & the Florida Keys
Las Vegas
Lima (Peru)
London
Los Angeles
Louisville
Marseille
Martha's Vineyard
Memphis
Mérida (Mexico)
Mexico City
Miami & South Beach
Milwaukee
Napa Valley

Naples & Marco Island
Nashville
New Orleans
Newport (R.I.)
New York / Manhattan
Paris
Philadelphia
Portland (Ore.)
Provincetown
San Diego
San Juan
Savannah
Seattle
Tampa Bay

CPSIA information can be obtained
at www.ICGtesting.com
Printed in the USA
LVHW011734230519
618889LV00012B/502

9 781641 872003